THE LIBRARY OF
AMERICAN
LIVES AND TIMES™

ROBERT ROGERS

Rogers' Rangers and the French and Indian War

Jennifer Quasha

The Rosen Publishing Group's
PowerPlus Books™
New York

To Keeks, another American hero

Published in 2002 by The Rosen Publishing Group, Inc.
29 East 21st Street, New York, NY 10010

First Edition

*Editor's Note: All quotations have been reproduced as they appeared in the
letters and diaries from which they were borrowed. No correction was made
to the inconsistent spelling or usage that was common in that time period.*

Library of Congress Cataloging-in-Publication Data

Quasha, Jennifer.
Robert Rogers : Rogers' Rangers and the French and Indian War /
Jennifer Quasha. — 1st ed.
    — (The library of American lives and times)
Includes bibliographical references and index.
ISBN 0-8239-5731-4
1. Rogers, Robert, 1731–1795—Juvenile literature. 2. Soldiers—United
States—Biography—Juvenile literature. 3. Rogers' Rangers—Juvenile
literature. 4. United States—History—French and Indian War,
1755–1763—Juvenile literature. [1. Rogers, Robert, 1731–1795. 2. Soldiers.
3. Rogers' Rangers. 4. United States—History—French and Indian War,
1755–1763.] I. Title. II. Series.
E199 .R749 2002
973.2'6'092—dc21

                                                            00-012985

Manufactured in the United States of America

CONTENTS

CARTE
DES POSSESSIONS
ANGLOISES & FRANÇOISES
DU CONTINENT DE
l'AMÉRIQUE SEPTENTRIONALE.
1755.

Echelle.

Bermudes I.

Explication.

1. Introduction to Robert Rogers and the French and Indian War

The early eighteenth century was an important time in America. Balances of power were shifting. Boundaries between the colonies and nations were a matter of heated dispute. In the mid-1700s, a major eruption occurred over land ownership. It was called the French and Indian War. The French and Indian War, also called the Great War for the Empire, was officially fought between 1754 and 1763 and it changed the map of the United States. In Britain, the French and Indian War is also called the Seven Years War because it lasted for seven years. England and France had been waging smaller battles for power against one another for seventy-five years. However, by 1754 it had exploded into the bloodiest war ever fought on American soil.

In the early eighteenth century, the French had settled in what is now Canada, in the Great Lakes

Opposite: This is a North American map of French and British colonial possessions in 1755. Throughout the eighteenth century, the French and British fought over land in North America, which served as a continuation of the wars that had been fought between the two countries for centuries in Europe.

region, and down the Mississippi River Valley into Louisiana. The British were living in colonies on the eastern shore of North America. Both France and Britain claimed to have discovered North America and therefore felt they had the rights to the land. Finally, England's king, George II, and France's king, Louis XV, realized they would need to fight for North America.

Although the American Revolutionary War, which followed shortly after the French and Indian War, is more widely recognized, the French and Indian War actually took more human lives. The French and Indian War was very important because, after Britain's victory,

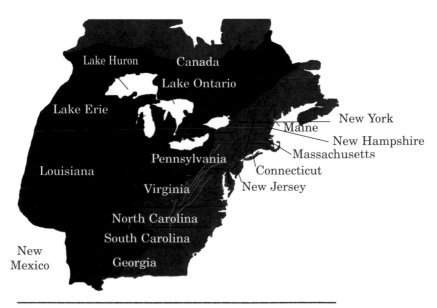

This map clearly shows the various territories that had been settled by the French and the English at the time of the French and Indian War. Notice that British territory did not extend beyond the Appalachian Mountains. The orange area depicts British territory, the purple area depicts French territory and the brown area depicts territory that the French and British were in dispute over. Grey lines show mountain regions.

the British took control of Canada. Ever since the British had arrived on the eastern shore of North America in the early 1600s, they had been creeping farther west and taking more and more land for themselves. Up until the 1700s, however, the Appalachian Mountains had limited British expansion.

The French and Indian War is so named because the British eventually won the war and they fought it against the French and their allies, the American Indians. If the French had won, perhaps it would today be known as the British War! However, it is important to realize that the British also were allied with the Indians. The Indians were very shrewd and played the French and the British against each other to help in their own territorial wars with neighboring Indians. The French were actually penetrating deeper into the continent, and into the Indians' land. However, the British established larger and more permanent settlements and the Indians viewed them as more of a threat.

Robert Rogers, a British Hero

One of the most famous figures in the French and Indian War was a man named Robert Rogers. He was born and raised in America, as a British subject. Throughout the French and Indian War, Robert Rogers led a group of men known as the Rangers. The Rangers were one of the most successful parts of the British attack on the French.

For the first part of the war, the British were losing badly to the French and their Indian allies. The British army had never encountered an enemy like the Indians. The British found it difficult to fight in their usual way in the rough wilderness of North America. The Indians took advantage of this by ambushing the British, launching quick attacks, and retreating into the familiar forests. The British could not compete fighting solely in their customary manner. Because Robert Rogers had been raised on North American soil, he not only knew the land on which the war was being fought, he also knew how to fight the Indians.

Robert Rogers, and other Rangers like him, played a big role in turning the tides. Ranger companies would take a more active role in the battles and they taught the British how to fight successfully against the Indians. If ranging companies like Rogers' Rangers had not fought for the British in the French and Indian War, it is possible that the British may never have won.

Opposite: This portrait of Robert Rogers is based on the 1776 engraving by Thomas Hart, published in London. Though the picture is not an authentic or accurate representation of Rogers, it is one of the best available. No known portraits of Rogers actually exist. The portrait is part of a series of engravings of American leaders, though Rogers was not an American (none of the colonists were at this time). All the pictures look very similar, making no real distinction between a Ranger uniform and a regular uniform.

2. Raising Robert Rogers

Robert Rogers was born on November 18, 1731, in Methuen, Massachusetts, a frontier town in the northeast of North America. Robert's parents, James and Mary Rogers, are thought to have immigrated, or moved, to America from Northern Ireland with their three children, Samuel, Daniel, and James. Not long after their arrival to North America, Robert, their fourth son, was born. After Robert's birth, they had another son, named Richard, and then in 1736 a daughter named Mary. James and Mary Rogers had six children altogether.

Some British settlers who were already living in New England, many of whom were Puritans, did not welcome settlers who were not Puritans themselves. They viewed all Irish and Scottish immigrants as Presbyterians or Roman Catholics and not to be tolerated. In fact, this prejudice or intolerance went so far that some communities even banned these settlers, so it was probably hard for the family to find a home.

Fortunately, in 1728, the community of Methuen let

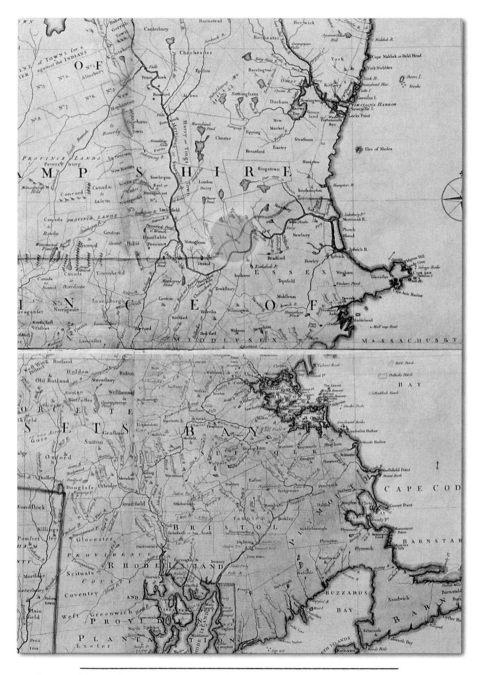

This eighteenth-century map shows the colonies of Massachusetts Bay, New Hampshire, Connecticut, and Rhode Island. The blue circle highlights Methuen, Massachusetts, the frontier town where Robert Rogers was born and spent a part of his childhood.

the Rogers family settle on land near the town's out-skirts. The Rogers family lived on that land for ten years. James and Mary struggled constantly to feed and clothe themselves and their children.

In 1738, the Rogerses purchased land farther north from the British government. Part of the Massachusetts Bay land grant, the land was called Great Meadow and later Mountalona. Thrilled to own their own land, they packed up everything they had. The Rogers family left Methuen, along with their neighbors the Pudneys, and walked up the Merrimack River with their cattle to land untouched by any European settlers. Their land was 10 miles (16 km) from the nearest community, so the two

This is a photograph of the Merrimack River, which was used by the Rogerses to guide them to their new home in northern Massachusetts. Many new settlers lived together for protection. Others, like the Rogerses, ventured far away from civilization to begin a new life.

families would be living in the North American wilderness practically alone. There was nothing but forest when they arrived. Anything they wanted, like a roof to shelter them, a barn to protect their animals, or a kitchen in which to cook their food, had to be created by their own labor.

Robert Rogers probably did not go to a formal school. He was needed to help out on his family's farm, and the nearest schools were too far away. Rogers learned to read and write well despite this lack of formal education.

The Rogers' only neighbors, besides the Pudneys, were the American Indians that lived nearby. Although Robert probably made friends with some of the neighboring Indians, many distrusted the English settlers because they had built homes on the Indians' land. Ever since the mid-1600s when British settlers began coming to North America in greater numbers, there had been fights between the Indians and British settlers. In fact, most of Robert's youth was spent under threat of attack from the Indians. Despite this, it is likely that Robert made friends with Indian children his same age. By living so close to and playing with the Indians, Robert learned how the Indians dressed, ate, lived, spoke, and, most importantly, how they fought. In fact, in his journals Robert Rogers wrote, "I could hardly avoid obtaining some knowledge of the manners, customs, and language of the Indians, as many of them resided in my neighborhood and daily conversed and dealt with the English."

In 1744, France declared war on Great Britain as a result of a larger European conflict, called the War for Austrian Succession. When this news arrived in North America, the French and British settlers started to skirmish, or have small fights, too. Up until this point, the British settlers had mainly settled on the eastern coast of North America and the French owned the land up north, which is now Canada. However, as more and more settlers came and spread out over the land the boundaries grew fuzzy. Both sides felt that their land rights were being threatened. Often these minor tensions were ignored by the leaders in Europe, and colonists were left to work things out for themselves. However, because the two countries were at war over in Europe, it was likely that these conflicts in North America would not be tolerated. The threat of an official attack began to build.

In 1745, when Robert was thirteen years old, French-led Indian attacks began in the English frontier. These assaults left British homes and villages pillaged and many were set on fire and destroyed. Many English women and children were captured, held prisoner, or killed by the Indians, while their husbands and fathers were brutally killed. The Rogers family, like other British settlers living in the wilderness, fled to the nearest city and sought protection in numbers. Local men were asked to join forces to stand up against the Indians. At age fourteen, Robert became a New Hampshire militiaman and joined the fight against the Indians.

This painting by John Edward Dunsmore illustrates an Indian attack on European homes. As Europeans began settling in North America, they often encountered resentment from various Native American tribes who were displaced by the new arrivals.

In 1748, tragedy struck the Rogers family. After ten years of hard work building a home and a farm of their own, a group of Indians raided the Rogers' home, setting fire to their crops and killing their animals. Their way of life was ruined. Robert Rogers was only seventeen years old.

As a militiaman and throughout his late teenage years, Rogers explored New Hampshire and its land. He traveled and talked to friendly Indians and hunters and learned the terrain. Robert Rogers grew up in the wilderness. By the time he was an adult, he loved it and knew how to survive in it.

Most adult settlers had to farm the land to make a living. This was one of Rogers' options, as well. However, it was not what Robert Rogers wanted to do. He wanted to explore the countryside, not stay in one place. It was what he had done since he was a child.

Not only did Rogers like to be in the wilderness, but he also had the physical qualities necessary to survive there. He was more than 6 feet (1.8 m) tall and he was strong. He had an excellent sense of direction and he always knew where he was in the woods. He also developed an eye for the terrain and could identify strange sounds. He was always willing to search deeper in the woods, where other people were afraid to go. Basically, Robert Rogers felt that the woods were his home.

In February 1755, Robert Rogers got himself in trouble. He was suspected of using counterfeit money, or money that was made illegally. He and fifteen other men were put on trial for their possible association with a local counterfeiting ring. Punishment for this crime was usually hanging until death, branding (when a mark was burned into the skin), or ear-clipping (when the bottom of the criminal's ear lobe was cut off).

Robert was scared, really scared. He would do anything to avoid being punished or killed. He sent a letter to a friend to whom he had also sent some counterfeit bills, and begged, "do the work you promised me" as "[my] life lays at your hands . . . once more I adjur you by your Maker to Do it or whie should such anonest man be Killed?" Luckily for him, Robert was helped by a justice of the peace whom he knew. The justice was named Joseph Blanchard. Blanchard was the commander of the New Hampshire Provincial Regiment. He needed men to join the fight against the French. Blanchard said if Robert Rogers would enlist in the volunteer army and help recruit other men, he could avoid being punished for his crime.

Not only was Robert very lucky to land this opportunity, but he was also the perfect man for the job.

3. The Scouting Rangers (1755–1756)

Robert Rogers was excited about the prospect of fighting. He knew the woods around him and he was happiest there, not in town. Rogers wrote in his journals: "My manner of life was such that it led me to a general acquaintance both with the British and French settlements in North America, and especially with the uncultivated forest, the mountains, valleys, rivers, lakes, and several passes that lay between . . . the settlements."

Rogers also knew many men he could recruit, or convince to join the army with him. By April 1755, at twenty-three years old, two months after he had narrowly escaped punishment, Rogers had become Captain Rogers. He had recruited fifty men to join his company, or group of soldiers. The first company of a regiment was traditionally the ranging company, which was the perfect company for Rogers to lead.

Robert Rogers' main job was scouting. This meant that Rogers would cross into enemy territory and take note of their numbers and what they were doing. He would then return to his own camp, report his findings to his superior, and plan ambushes. This was very important work because the British needed to know how many French and Indian soldiers were nearby in order to prepare for battle against them.

The British were losing to the French until this point. Although they had met with some success, the British did not know how to effectively battle the French-led Indians. Also, when a British soldier was asked to scout a French and Indian camp, the soldier often returned with little or no helpful information. Until ranging companies, most notably Rogers and his men, were given a more prominent role, rumors and fear were hurting the British army. The British imagined that there were far more French and Indian soldiers than there actually were. Once Rogers told the British army the reality of the situation, the army had the confidence to fight the French and fight well.

A Real Scouting Mission

On September 14, 1755, when darkness settled over the wilderness, Rogers and four men left their camp near Lake George in a bateau, or flat-bottomed boat. They were going to scout out the French fort at Crown Point, or as the French called it, Fort St. Frédéric. Rogers and his men, known as Rangers, traveled at night when they had less chance of being seen by their enemy. Once daylight broke they would come ashore, hide their boats, sleep, eat, and prepare until nightfall,

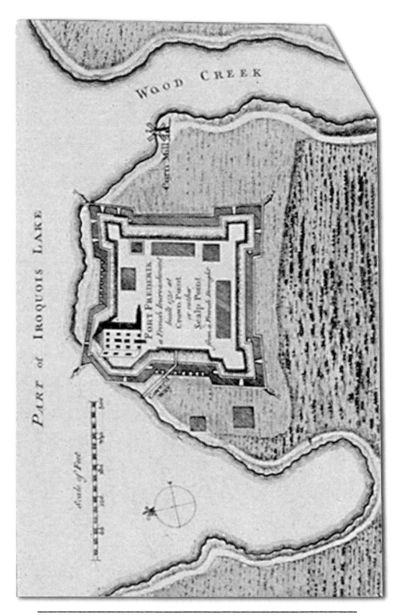

This is a plan of the French fort at Crown Point, which the French called Fort St. Frédéric. On September 22, 1731, the Marquis de Beauharnois, then governor general of Canada, erected the fort on Lake Champlain. Fort St. Frédéric was a small stockade with a garrison of only 30 men. By 1736 it had been enlarged, and could hold a garrison of 120 men. It was enlarged once more, and in 1742 was, with the exception of Quebec, the strongest work held by the French.

when they could continue their mission. Two and a half days after they left, Rogers and his Rangers arrived at Fort St. Frédéric.

Through the trees, they saw the gray walls of the French fort. A moat, or ditch, surrounded the walls of the fort and there was a drawbridge that could be laid across to allow people to cross. Inside the walls, Rogers saw tents, a church, and a stone citadel, or stronghold. Rogers also saw the enemy. There were five or six hundred French soldiers wearing white coats, and there were also Indians.

Rogers described this journey to Crown Point in his journals: "At night I crept through the enemy's guard into a small village lying south of the fort, and passing their centries to an eminence south-west of it, from whence I discovered they were building a battery, and had already thrown up an entrenchment on that side of the fort."

When night came, Rogers' Rangers headed back to camp carrying important knowledge about the enemy. Rogers had done such a good job scouting and bringing back information that he was asked to scout another French fort at Ticonderoga, called Fort Carillon.

After only three days of rest, Rogers and four Rangers left camp on the evening of September 27, 1755. Again they traveled under the cover of nightfall and rowed north on Lake George. During their dark trip down Lake George, they passed their enemy gath-

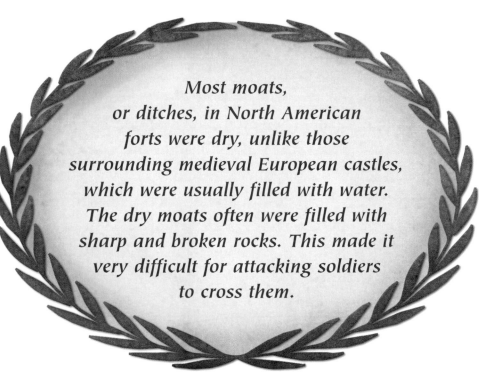

*Most moats,
or ditches, in North American
forts were dry, unlike those
surrounding medieval European castles,
which were usually filled with water.
The dry moats often were filled with
sharp and broken rocks. This made it
very difficult for attacking soldiers
to cross them.*

ered around campfires. Although the Rangers could see them, the French had no idea the Rangers were there.

Rogers' Rangers were far behind enemy lines. If they happened upon someone, that person would undoubtedly be the enemy.

After leaving three men behind with the canoes, Rogers and one man traveled through the forest to scout the French fort. They saw one camp, which held about one thousand French and Indians. Only 1.5 miles (2.4 km) away, Rogers and his men saw another camp with about three thousand French and Indians! Until Rogers saw the fort at Ticonderoga, the British army was uncertain just how many French were actually there.

This modern-day photograph by Lee Snider shows the south barracks at Fort Ticonderoga, now part of a museum.
Fort Ticonderoga would be the scene of many battles in the French and Indian War and later during the Revolutionary War.

Armed again with important knowledge, Rogers returned to the Rangers who had stayed behind with the canoes. Upon his arrival, the three men told him that an enemy canoe had just floated by! Instead of rushing back to the British fort in fear, Rogers told his men to hide and wait for the enemy canoe to return. Rogers planned to ambush the enemy canoe.

The Rangers lay in wait and watched the enemy canoe come closer and closer to their position on the shore. As the canoe paddled nearby, Rogers ordered his

This is an ink-on-glass portrait of Sir William Johnson. As the northern super-intendent of Indian affairs, Johnson was noted for his fair dealings with the Indians but was often ruthless and unscrupulous in his other affairs. Johnson later became one of Robert Rogers' worst enemies and the cause of many of his difficulties. Some historians feel this rivalry stemmed from the fact that Rogers was also popular with the American Indians and Johnson viewed him as competition.

men to shoot. The British fired, killing some of the French. The others paddled as hard as they could away from the Rangers, to safety. Though the noise from the gunfight brought three French canoes to help, it was too late. By the time the French backup had arrived, Rogers and his men had escaped.

This story of Rogers' bravery made him a hero. Not only had Rogers brought back valuable information, but he had been brave enough to attack the enemy in enemy territory. Rogers' superior, a man named William Johnson, exclaimed to three governors back in the British colonies, "I believe him to be as brave & as honest a Man as any I have equal knowledge of, & both myself & all the Army are convinced that he has distinguished himself since he has been among us." Newspapers in the colonies began writing about Rogers and people started to remember this hero's name.

Rogers' Success

Why was Rogers so successful? Besides being brave and willing to fight for his country, he knew how to fight in the wilderness of North America like the Indians did. He knew how to move among the trees, swamps, and thick bushes, and when it was time to attack or to retreat. He was a master of the ambush. He knew the value of surprise and knew that it was important to stay hidden until the enemy was close before jumping up and shooting. This took a great deal of patience and bravery.

Before Rogers joined their ranks, the British soldiers often marched toward the enemy in a wide line next to fife players and drummers announcing the attack. This type of fighting did not always work well in America's landscape. The British soldiers needed to change the way they fought.

Rogers had men spread out to cover specific areas in the front, in the middle, and at the rear of his party. Because the men were spread out this way, it was difficult for the enemy to surround them or to judge their numbers. It also allowed them to cover more ground in their scouting missions. All of his men needed to be brave because they were often alone, or in groups of two or three, in different areas of the woods. That is why they were called Rangers. Instead of marching in lines, the troops ranged through the forest.

Not only did Rogers know how to fight like the Indians, but he could teach the British how to do it, too.

Training the Rangers

Rogers had to train and drill his Rangers. They had to learn how to be soldiers. First, Rogers' men needed to know how to keep themselves as clean and healthy as possible, a difficult task while living in camps in the wilderness for long periods of time. They also needed to dress appropriately for fighting in the woods. Clothing had to hug the body so that it would not get caught in the thick shrubs. The Rangers also wore either leather shoes

The Battle of Lexington, April 19 1775. Plate 1

This is a painting of the Battle of Lexington, which happened years later, but it shows clearly the standard formation in which the British army fought. In the dense woods of North America, British troops could not maintain their formations. They often were defeated by the Indians, and later by the colonists who had grown up in the American landscape and attacked from behind trees and rocks.

or Indian-style moccasins. They wore leather or woolen leggings to protect their legs from the underbrush.

They needed to know how to walk quietly through dense forests as well as wide-open spaces, and to run whenever necessary, sometimes for long periods of time. They also needed to know and follow Rogers' commands immediately and without question.

This 1759 painting was created by Thomas Davies, who lived from 1737 through 1812. It provides a view of the lines at Lake George in 1759. The painting is believed to depict a Ranger at work. This is the only known period illustration of a Ranger at work. The Indian in the painting was most likely a Stockbridge Indian Ranger.

Rogers also trained the Rangers to handle their weapons and fire them while standing up, kneeling, and lying on the ground. They had to learn how to load, aim, and fire their guns quickly and quietly. They could not waste valuable seconds reloading; every bullet needed to find its mark. There was no time for careless mistakes.

Along with these basic tasks, the Rangers needed to be able to swim, sometimes while holding their weapons and ammunition above their heads. They had to be able to dodge trees while running, dig trenches to hide in, cut down trees to make forts, saw logs for campfire wood, make canoes that stayed afloat, build bridges, hunt animals for food, and even mend their uniforms with a needle and thread if they were torn.

Being a Ranger was not easy. The men who were successful would master all the skills Rogers taught them. The ones who couldn't would not survive in the wilderness or in the battles against the French and Indians.

Rogers' training was so unique and useful that he was asked to commit it to paper. What he created were "Rogers' Rules of Ranging," a list of rules that would change the way battles were fought. Although he probably did not create all of the rules, he was the first man to write them down and is therefore given credit for their creation. "Rogers' Rules of Ranging" were not only useful in the eighteenth century; they are still being used today.

JOURNALS

OF

Major ROBERT ROGERS:

CONTAINING

An Account of the feveral Excurfions he made under the Generals who commanded upon the Continent of NORTH AMERICA, during the late War.

From which may by collected

The moft material Circumftances of every Campaign upon that Continent, from the Commencement to the Conclufion of the War.

LONDON:

Printed for the AUTHOR,
And fold by J. MILLAN, Bookfeller, near Whitehall.
MDCCLXV.

Robert Rogers' published Journals offered people on both sides of the Atlantic a window into the French and Indian War. It earned Rogers fame and renown. However, even with this success he was still not able to escape from his debts.

4. Not Everybody Liked the Rangers (1757–1758)

Robert Rogers and his Rangers were unique because they were able to blend the techniques used by the Indians to fight in the wilderness, but also had qualities of the British soldier and understood the importance of tactics and discipline. Some people, however, felt Rogers was more like an Indian than a British soldier. He not only fought like the Indians, but he also dressed like them and carried the same weapons, such as a scalping knife and a tomahawk. It was because of these things that he was so successful in the war and important to the British.

However, Robert Rogers was different than the British, and this caused some of them to mistrust and misunderstand him. Although many British did support his men and their way of fighting, this lack of trust by the others plagued Rogers throughout his military career. Nevertheless, they let him fight because he was helping them win the war.

Robert Rogers was born and raised in America. This made him different than the British people who came to the colonies as adults. Families like Rogers' had left

Robert Rogers learned a great deal about fighting from the Native American tribes he came in contact with as a child. Above we can see an illustration of a Ranger, at left, and a Stockbridge Indian warrior at right. Notice their similar styles of dress. Rogers purposely copied many of these styles because he realized that certain types of clothing were better suited to fighting in the wilderness.

Britain for a new land. Once in America, they had to survive under harsh conditions, which made them rough and tough. They were starting to develop into a different and independent people. Some of the British found this hard to accept or understand. Just because they lived in America and its vast wilderness, the Rangers seemed rude and hard to the British.

The Rangers' dress, fighting technique, and often-unruly behavior while they were at camp hurt their reputation even more. The most famous example of the "uncouth" Rangers became known as the Mutiny of the Whipping Post.

The Mutiny of the Whipping Post

For some of the war, Rogers' Rangers lived on Rogers Island, a camp at Fort Edward in the middle of the Hudson River. On this island, there was a whipping post where disobedient soldiers were punished. The offending soldier was tied to the post and flogged.

In December 1757, a group of Rangers revolted against the practice of being punished at the whipping post. These men caused a mutiny. The mutiny was started because two Rangers had been whipped for stealing rum and other men felt the punishment was unfair.

Following spread: This is a reconstruction of a plan of Fort Edward as it looked in 1759, during Rogers' time. The island directly across from the fort was called Rogers Island because it was used by Rogers to train his men for battle. The Rangers stayed in log huts. The island also housed a military barracks, a military hospital and a smallpox hospital.

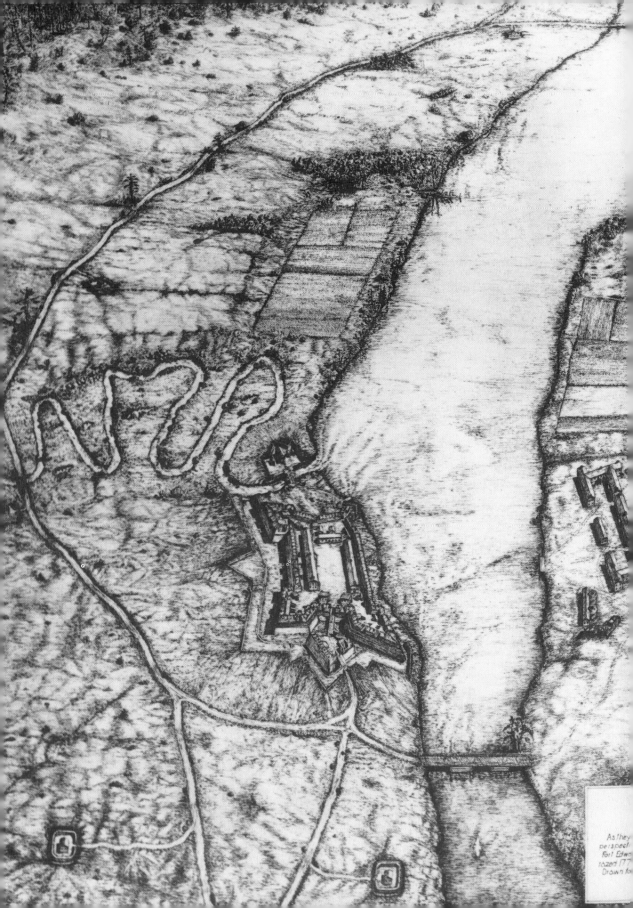

They threatened to knock down the whipping post, saying if men continued to be flogged they would rebel or desert the company altogether.

Amid a loud ruckus, six Rangers surrounded the whipping post while one cut it down with an ax. Upon hearing the noise, other Rangers appeared, but they did not know what to do. Should they join in, run away, or try to stop them? All they knew was that they did not want to get into trouble. Finally the mutineers were controlled and imprisoned by the officers in charge.

This type of disorder among Rangers threatened the unity and trust shared within the group, and that was dangerous. Rangers needed to trust each other and work together to survive. If certain men were unwilling to play by the rules, innocent men could get hurt. Rogers was forced to speak with his superiors, or bosses, about this mutiny. He wanted to settle the problem without making anybody unhappy.

Rogers did not want men who did not take part in the mutiny to be punished. He was concerned that Rangers might choose to desert, or leave the company, if they were punished without cause. However, Rogers knew that something had to be done to ease the British army's fear that the Rangers were out of control. One of Rogers' superiors wanted to hang the man who had caused the mutiny, but Rogers convinced him to dismiss all the offending men from the service instead.

Although the result of this mutiny was not drastic,

it hurt the Rangers' reputation. All of Rogers' enemies who accused the Rangers of being vicious, disobedient, and uncontrollable now had more ammunition to use against them.

Rangers Uniforms and Equipment

There was no set uniform when the Rangers first began serving in the French and Indian War in 1755. The Rangers all brought their own clothing from home and wore it to fight. Rogers knew that the best type of clothing for his Rangers was similar to what the Indians wore. It was important that the Rangers' clothes fit snugly around their bodies, so that when they ran through the woods, the clothes did not catch on trees and branches. The Rangers' legs also needed to be protected so that the thorns and bushes that they had to walk through would not scratch their legs and cause wounds.

Unlike other companies in the British army who stopped fighting during the cold northeast winters, the Rangers continued scouting and fighting. Therefore their clothing also needed to keep them warm. Each Ranger had at least two blankets that they had either brought from home or that in later years were given to them by the army. Blankets were some of the most important items that the Rangers had. In the winter, some blankets were cut and sewn together to make hooded blanket-coats. Men also often wrapped another blanket around their bodies, on top of the blanket-coats.

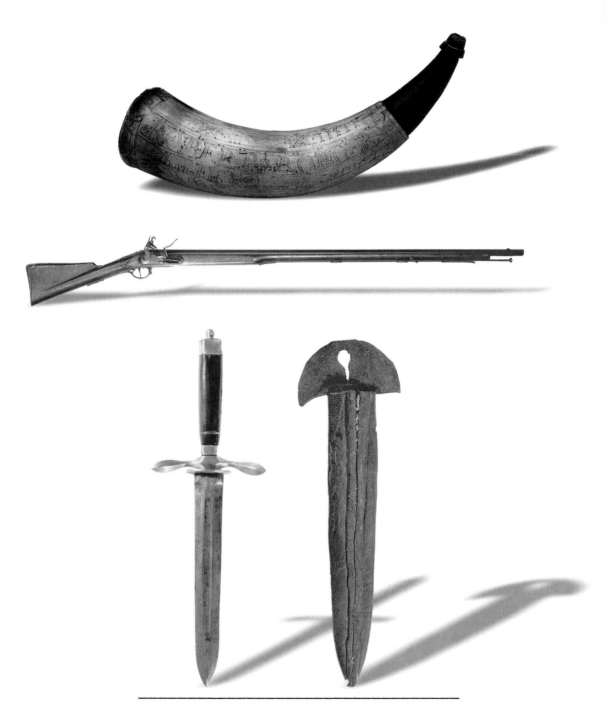

Above is Robert Rogers' actual powderhorn and a typical gun used by Rangers at the time. The knife (bottom left) and sheath (bottom right) are also from the time and typical of the kind that Indians and the Rangers would have used.

The Rangers used their blankets like sleeping bags in camp, and always had them when they went out to fight or scout. To protect their necks, ears, and faces, Rangers wore gloves, scarves, and hats made from bear skin.

The Rangers carried a rectangular pouch with a flap, called a haversack. It was suspended over their shoulders by a strap. The haversack contained provisions, or food, like cornmeal and dried beef chips, a tin plate, a spoon, and a horn mug. Some Rangers hid a flask, or bottle, of poisoned rum in their packs. They hoped that in the event that they were killed or taken prisoner, their enemy, when finding the rum, would drink it and die. For their own safe use, each Ranger carried a canteen, which held a supply of water, and which hung at their side by a strap over the shoulder. When they were desperate for food, the Rangers also knew how to pick lily roots and which berries and bugs were safe to eat.

In 1756, Rogers' Rangers were given ten Spanish dollars by the British government to buy more appropriate clothing. They finally would have their own uniforms.

On top the Rangers wore hunting shirts made of cloth, usually of wool or linen. On their legs Rangers wore breeches of wool or linen. On top of their breeches, Rangers often wore wool or leather leggings, similar to the ones worn by the Indians. These wool leggings laced up the sides of their pant legs from the ankles to the middle of their thighs and protected them from insects, snakes, bushes, thorns, and anything that might hurt their legs. On their feet, Rangers often wore moccasins, which they first learned about from the Indians. Moccasins were made of leather and were much warmer than the shoes people wore in Britain. Keeping their heads covered also helped Rangers stay warm in the cold weather. Rangers wore Scottish bonnets made from wool, which were sometimes decorated with a small tuft of bear fur.

At first, in 1755, Rangers brought their own weapons from home. Usually they brought a firelock, or musket, and a hatchet or an ax. Their ammunition consisted of sixty rounds of powder and ball. Powder was carried in a powder horn, and ball was kept in a leather bag. Powder and ball were loaded together into the musket.

In 1758, Rogers requested better weapons for his Rangers. He ordered muskets that were lighter to carry, shorter, and therefore less visible to the enemy, and that had bayonets, or knives, on the end of them for use when the Rangers were fighting face-to-face with their enemy. The barrels were brown so that they would not catch the sun's glare on sunny days and alert the enemy to their position.

On a strap looped over their shoulders, Rangers also carried a powder horn that hung near their waists. The horn, which was often carved and decorated by the Rangers, held gunpowder that was poured down the barrel and in the touch-hole on the side of their musket. When the Ranger squeezed the trigger, a flint striking

This picture illustrates a man loading a gun using a powder horn. Rogers' men had to practice loading their guns very quickly so no time would be lost during a battle where surprise and timing were of the essence.

a piece of steel made the powder catch fire and propelled bullets at the enemy. Each Ranger carried a leather or sealskin pouch at their waist. The pouch held ammunition for their muskets.

Each Ranger had a tomahawk, or ax, which they used not only in battle but also in camp to chop wood. The head of the tomahawk was made from steel and the handle was made from wood. One correct swing of the tomahawk at an enemy standing an arm's length away could deliver a fatal blow when contact was made.

Along with their tomahawks, Rangers had a scalping knife, or a long, thin hunting knife, which was used in close fighting to remove the enemy's scalp. "Scalping" was a popular practice in the French and Indian War. Bringing many enemy scalps back to camp was seen as tough, courageous, and brave. The scalping knife was used to make a circular cut on the head, or scalp, of the enemy. Then the hair and scalp were ripped off. Both the Indians and Europeans used the painful and vicious practice during the war.

This illustration shows the French soldiers and their Indian allies scalping English prisoners after the capture of William Henry. The picture is from a 1761 book, *The Cruel Massacre of the Protestants in North-America: Shewing How the French and Indians Joined Together to Scalp the English, and the Manner of their Scalping*. The book was printed in London to raise public sentiment against the French and Indians. In reality, the brutal practice of scalping was carried on by both the English and the French.

5. The Rangers, the Battle on Snowshoes, and Lord Howe (1758–1759)

In the middle of 1757, Lord George Augustus Viscount Howe was made a brigadier in North America. Lord Howe was a big fan of Rogers and his Rangers. He suggested to the other troops under his command that they learn and copy the style of fighting that the Rangers employed. This was an important moment in Rogers' military career. Although other officers had supported him before, Lord Howe was the first high-ranking officer who was not only openly supportive of the way Rogers and his Rangers fought, but also wanted other soldiers to learn Ranger tactics.

Rogers' Rock and the Battle on Snowshoes

In 1758, Colonel William Haviland asked Rogers' Rangers to be a part of the attack on the French fort at Ticonderoga, the same fort that Rogers had scouted in 1755. Rogers agreed. Despite some concerns about security issues, this was one of the largest British efforts thus far, and he wanted to be a part of it.

This is a portrait of Viscount George Augustus Howe wearing the uniform of the 1st guards. It is believed to have been painted between 1723 and 1792. Howe was a great supporter of Robert Rogers and his Rangers before his death in July 1758.

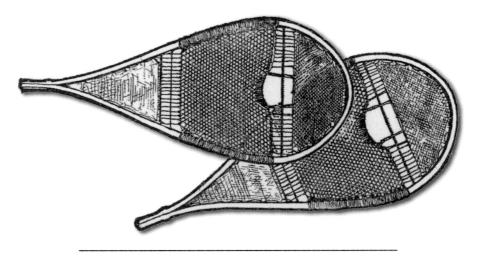

Snowshoes were a very important part of several battles between the French and British forces. Each side kept fighting during the harsh winter months.

On March 10, 1758, Rogers' Rangers, in new crisp uniforms, left Rogers Island near Fort Edward. They joined other Rangers and British soldiers in a combined force of 180 men and headed north toward Ticonderoga. It was still winter, and the soldiers and Rangers wore snowshoes, which allowed for easier travel over ice and deep snow. They marched north, wrapping their blankets tightly around them for warmth.

After three days, Rogers' men were in enemy territory and were only two miles (3.2 km) from Fort Carillon at Ticonderoga. Rogers had an uneasy feeling gnawing at him, and it turned out that he had good reason for it. Soon, Ranger scouts informed him that the enemy was coming toward them, walking over an icy

Captain James Abercrombie was a talented British officer who sometimes scouted with the Rangers. He was a relative of General James Abercromby, who was also friendly with Robert Rogers. The exact relationship between Abercrombie and Abercromby is unclear. It can be confusing when reading letters and accounts of Rogers' activities, because he has dealings with both men. An easy rule to follow is that the captain always spelled his name Abercrombie, and the general always spelled his Abercromby.

stream. The scouts were only partially correct. Actually the enemy was everywhere.

Suddenly, Indians in war paint attacked from behind bushes and trees. Robert Rogers fired his weapon to warn his party, but the brutal fighting had already begun. More enemy soldiers appeared from what seemed like nowhere, and more and more Rangers went down. The French and Indians attacked from all sides. Rogers' Rangers fought bravely, but few survived the surprise attack.

Legend has it that Robert Rogers, while fleeing the attacking French, put on his snowshoes and skied down a huge snow-covered rock at the edge of Lake George, barely escaping the enemy close behind him. In the middle of his flight, Rogers took off his jacket, tossed it to the ground, and left it behind. Upon finding his jacket, the French thought that they had finally killed the infamous British warrior they had been trying to kill for years. Elated, the French returned to camp and celebrated Rogers' death. Little

This painting by Jean Leon Gerome Ferris is titled *Battle of Rogers' Rock*. The battle, also known as the Battle on Snowshoes, was a major defeat for the British and the worst defeat of Rogers' entire career in the British army. Although this is the best and most well known painting of the battle, it is historically inaccurate. The Ranger dress is incorrect, and the soldier, meant to be British, is in an American uniform from the Revolutionary War. Nonetheless, we do get a feeling of what it was like to be fighting in the wilderness.

did they know that Robert Rogers was still very much alive! Today, that rock is known as Rogers' Rock and the battle is known as the Battle on Snowshoes. Although Rogers survived, the British were crushed. Only 54 of the 180 men survived. Robert Rogers was devastated. He had suffered the worst defeat of his career.

Captain James Abercrombie tried to comfort Rogers after the loss of so many of his men. He said, "It is better to die with the reputation of a brave man, fighting for his country in a good cause, than either shamefully running away to preserve one's life, or lingering about in old age, and dying in one's bed, without having done his country or his King any service."

6. Abercromby, Amherst, and Britain's Big Push North (1758–1759)

On April 6, 1758, shortly after his return from Ticonderoga, Robert Rogers heard that he had been promoted from captain to major, a rank he had wanted for some time.

During that same spring, the British were planning a major move north to attack the French. British forces were called upon to attack three major areas: Louisbourg, Fort Duquesne, and Ticonderoga and Crown Point. Howe and Rogers' Rangers were part of the British army that would attack the last area, Ticonderoga and Crown Point. Beginning that April in 1758, Rogers worked closely with his Rangers, scouting and preparing them for battle. Rogers wanted to make sure they won.

Early in the morning on July 5, 1758, fifteen thousand Rangers and British soldiers left Fort Edward on Lake George, in more than one thousand boats, to travel north. With the Rangers' boats in the

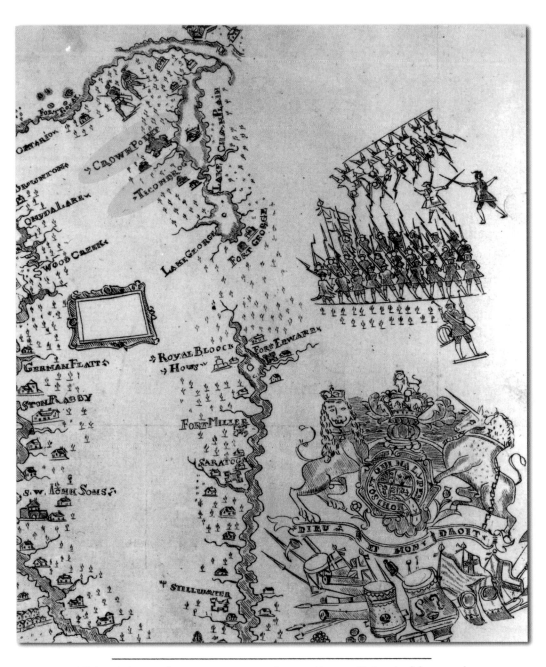

This eighteenth-century map shows Crown Point in blue and Ticonderoga in green. The British focused a lot of energy trying to recapture these two key forts during the French and Indian War.

lead, after a day of travel, the boats pulled onto the enemy shore. While the one thousand British boats were lifted to safety and a temporary camp was made, the Rangers went ahead to scout on foot. Lord Howe and his men followed. Suddenly, Howe's group came upon nearly three hundred French soldiers that seemed to appear out of nowhere. Firelocks exploded from both sides, and immediately the British army sprang into action. The Rangers turned around when they heard the firing and attacked the French from the rear. Although it did not take long for the British to surround the French and kill many of them, the French had already delivered one devastating blow. Lord Howe had caught an enemy bullet and was instantly killed.

Lord Howe's death literally froze the British army in place. That evening they remained in their makeshift camp in the forest. They had no idea how to proceed without their leader. British morale was low and they sat stunned, mourning the loss of their favorite leader.

The following morning, General Abercromby, Howe's superior, ordered the British army back to

On the following spread: This eighteenth-century map was drawn to show the plan of attack that was used by Major General Abercromby and his men as they attacked Ticonderoga. It depicts the position of the rear guard formed by the Connecticut and New Jersey troops, and also shows the position of the Rangers, bateaux men, or soldiers in boats, that guarded the waterways, and the infantry.

The ATTACK of

TICONDEROGA;

MAJOR GENERAL ABERCROMBY

COMMANDER in CHIEF.

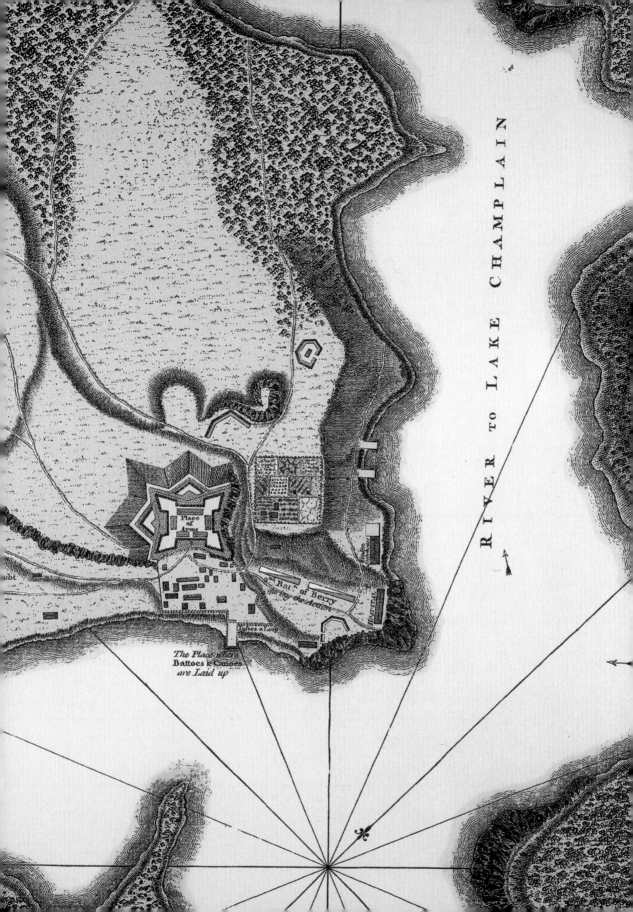

Place
of
Arms

R^d Batⁿ of Berry

The Place where
Battoes & Canoes
are Laid up

RIVER TO LAKE CHAMPLAIN

The French soldiers that Howe's men came upon were led by Jean-Baptiste Levrault de Langis Montegron. The French had been watching Howe approach from Bald Mountain, or Rogers' Rock, and got lost in the woods while trying to get back to Ticonderoga to warn the French and Indians of the British attack. Montegron was one of the best leaders the French had and one of Rogers' biggest rivals, yet he and his men got lost in what was basically their own backyard!

camp. Abercromby, deeply affected by the loss of Lord Howe, decided that the British needed to retreat and regroup. Many soldiers criticized General Abercromby for his lack of leadership and for his indecision in this crisis.

The effect of Lord Howe's death stunned the British soldiers and James Abercromby's indecision enabled the French army to strengthen their fortifications. When Abercromby sent the British army back to fight, the French had already prepared for the attack. This attack left two thousand more British dead. The British suffered a big defeat. On July 9, only four days after they left, the soldiers retreated back to the south end of Lake George.

The highlight of Jeffrey Amherst's military career was during the French and Indian War. He was later made commander in chief of the British army because of his performance. However, he was not very successful in this position and was heavily criticized. This 1780 cartoon published by H. Humphrey criticized Amherst for his lack of leadership and his tendency to take a back seat in the wars he commanded. In part, the cartoon reads "There you see the generals without orders. . . ."

In December 1758, Jeffrey Amherst took over for General Abercromby. While Abercromby's men were being crushed by the French, Amherst had led the British to victory at Louisbourg. Like Howe, General Amherst respected and appreciated Rogers' Rangers and he also wanted them at his side.

In 1759, the British tried again to launch a three-level fight against the French. Amherst tried to take the French Fort Carillon at Ticonderoga, and two other generals attacked Fort Niagara and Quebec. Amherst

This photograph shows all that is left of Fort George today (it is also visible on the map on page 50). Amherst had sent Rogers and his men to create a stronghold here but the action of the war would soon take them elsewhere and the fort would never be finished.

vowed that this time the British army would not lose. General Amherst sent his men, along with Rogers' Rangers, to build a strong fort near Lake George, called Fort George. Amherst's men set out for battle from this spot, but in the end, Fort George would never be finished.

On July 22, 1759, the British army left Fort George. Again, Rogers and his men led the way. By the next morning the British had surrounded Fort Carillon's outskirts. On July 26, Rogers was sent closer to the fort's walls to cut through and remove a log boom, or barrier, that the French had placed across a narrow part of Lake Champlain to block the British approach.

As Rogers approached the log boom, Fort Carillon exploded. Flames shot through the sky. The French destroyed their own fort, admitted defeat, and fled down Lake Champlain. Rogers' Rangers chased the French boats and caught ten of them. The British were able to retrieve many French goods from the boats and the burning fort, including ammunition. After many failed attempts, the British finally had control of Ticonderoga.

This 1867 hand-colored steel engraving shows Lake Champlain. It was done by R. Hinshelwood from a picture by D. Johnson. Rogers and his Rangers knew the area around Lake Champlain very well and were used to scout and plan ambushes here throughout the war.

Some of Amherst's men stopped to rebuild the fort at Ticonderoga. Others, along with the Rangers, went to look for the French soldiers who had fled and to scout Fort St. Frédéric near Crown Point. It happened that the fleeing French had stayed at Fort St. Frédéric only long enough to blow that fort up, too!

Finally, after years of trying to get Fort Carillon at Ticonderoga and Fort St. Frédéric at Crown Point, the British took control of both French forts. The British at last governed the Champlain Valley.

7. Robert Rogers' Attack on St. Francis (1759)

In September 1759, two British soldiers from Amherst's group were sent to find out how the British attack on Quebec was going. These two soldiers were captured midroute by Abenaki Indians. Amherst was enraged and wanted to retaliate, or get back at the Indians responsible.

On September 12, Amherst asked Rogers to prepare 220 men for battle. Each man was given rations, or food, for thirty days. They were going to launch a secret attack on the Indian village of St. Francis. Before the Rangers left, Amherst said to them: "Remember the barbarities that have been committed by the enemy's Indian scoundrels on every occasion, where they had an opportunity of shewing their infamous cruelties on the King's subjects, which they have done without mercy. Take your revenge, but don't forget that tho' those villains have dastardly and promiscuously murdered the women and children of all ages, it is my orders that no women or children are killed or hurt . . ."

The Abenaki Indians were responsible for much of the

carnage on the New York and New England frontier, and possibly for the attack on the Rogers family farm. Rogers and many other Rangers had a strong urge to retaliate.

On September 13, 1759, Rogers set out with his men from Crown Point on a long voyage north. He knew it would be a difficult journey. Not only would he and his men have to cover 150 miles (241.4 km) of unknown wilderness to get to St. Francis, they also would have to pass through the French-controlled Lake Champlain to get there. They left at nightfall and traveled under cover of darkness. While in enemy territory, they kept their rowing as quiet as they could. Other Rangers listened for even the slightest sound that might signal an enemy. When daylight came they went ashore, hid their boats, scouted the area to make sure it was safe, and rested until dusk. Already the trip had been tough on the Rangers. Within six days of setting off, Rogers lost more than forty men to illness and injury. The rest of the Rangers pressed on.

The weather turned against them. It began to rain and navigating the boats was difficult. The Rangers fought to stay healthy and dry. On September 23, the Rangers, numbering less than two hundred men, landed on shore and left their boats under the watch of two Stockbridge Indians. They planned to return to their boats after the attack on St. Francis, but at this point it was best to travel on foot.

Two days later, the two men who had been left with the boats ran panting into camp, exhausted. The two brave Rangers had been running for hours. The French had found them and had burned all of their boats! In fact, the French were not far behind them.

Rogers remained calm. He realized then that the Rangers would not be able to return the way they had planned. Instead, they would have to return by a much longer route. Rogers immediately sent Lieutenant Andrew McMullen, who had been injured, to tell Amherst of their change of plan. Rogers also requested that Amherst send food to a rendezvous point at the junction of the Wells and Connecticut Rivers, north of

This is a photograph of British Fort No. 4, where Rogers went to get supplies for his starving men after their attack on St. Francis. Fort No. 4 was a very old civilian fort that was so called because at one time it was in Township No. 4 of the Massachusetts Bay Colony.

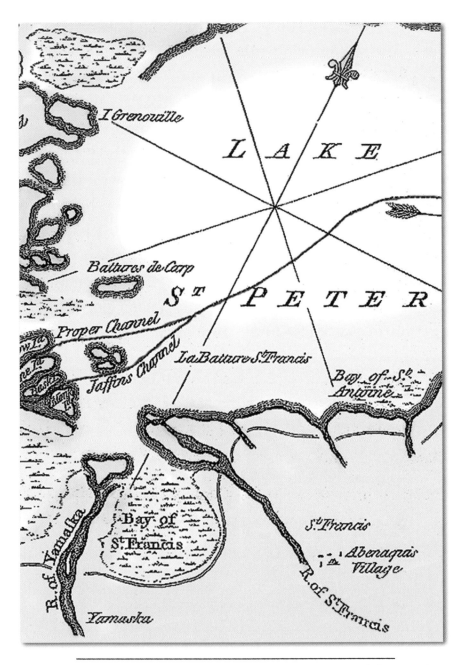

This map by T. Kitchin shows the St. Francis River and the nearby Abenaki Village. This is the area in which Robert Rogers and his Rangers planned their retaliation raid against the Abenaki village where the British soldiers had been captured as they traveled to Quebec.

the British fort called No. 4. Rogers knew that after such a long trip they would need the food desperately.

To avoid the pursuing French, the Rangers quickly set out again. This time it was not the weather, but the wilderness, that turned against them. For days the Rangers had to wade through cold, muddy swampland. Because they had stomped through thick, dirty water for so long, their feet were tender and covered with painful sores. The endless bog also prohibited the Rangers from lighting a fire to warm themselves. The tired, soaking-wet Rangers tripped on weeds hidden in the mud, and fell face-first into the swamp. They were exhausted from lack of sleep. Their only food was the dried beef and cornmeal they carried in their haversacks.

Finally, nine days later, they made it through the swamp and stood on hard ground. However, it was not long before they had to cross the icy, five-foot-deep St. Francis River. The men clung to each other so they were not swept away by the river's frigid current. It took every ounce of strength the Rangers had left to cross safely. Once on the opposite shore they still had 15 miles (24 km) to go. By that time, most men were out of food.

On October 5, the Rangers were close to St. Francis. Some Rangers waited behind while others went to scout out the Indian village. Then Rogers and his scouts returned to report that they had found the Indians "in high frolic or dance," or having what looked like a party.

The 141 remaining Rangers waited until early the next morning before attacking. While they were waiting just 1,500 yards (1,372 m) away from the village, Rogers gave the Rangers their orders. Guns were to be loaded, the ties of their tomahawks loosened, their haversacks laid aside, and their bayonets firmly attached to the tip of their firelocks. The orders were simple: The Rangers were to kill the men and take the women and children.

Leaving their backpacks behind, the Rangers crept into the sleeping village. Just as dawn broke, they attacked the unsuspecting inhabitants. Most of the Indians were dead before they even knew what was happening. Those that tried to escape were caught easily because they were tired and groggy from the party the night before. The hungry Rangers took some corn from the Indians' supply but took little else before they set the village on fire.

By seven o'clock in the morning the raid was done. The Rangers guessed that they had killed at least two hundred men, although the actual number was probably lower. They took twenty women and children as prisoners. Five of the women were Englishwomen who had been captured and held prisoner by the Indians.

It was time to move on. The Rangers had a lot of distance to cover before they found their food at the rendezvous point where the Connecticut and the Wells Rivers meet. The terrain homeward did not get easier, and the weather was against them again. The Rangers had to climb rocky mountains and trudge through muddy swamps while freezing rain poured from the sky.

On October 13, when they were still a great distance away from the rendezvous point, the Rangers decided to split up and travel in smaller groups. Fewer than two days after they parted ways, one of the groups again caught up to Rogers. Their group had run into the enemy and seven men had been taken.

By this time, the Rangers were out of food and they had little strength with which to search and kill animals for food. They ate mostly leaves, mushrooms, and roots for energy. Starvation was a bigger concern than the French soldiers and Indians who could possibly be lurking in the wilderness. By October 20, the Rangers still had 60 miles (95 km) to travel to reach the rendezvous point.

Amherst had arranged for food to be at the rendezvous point, sending Lieutenant Samuel Stephens to head the relief party and bring the food. Stephens waited at the rendezvous point for two days until he heard a gunshot. Fearing it was the French, he and his party left, taking all the food with them.

Rogers had fired his gun to let the relief party know that they were close. When the Rangers arrived, no one was there. Rogers wrote in his journals: "Our distress upon this occasion was truly inexpressible; our spirits, greatly depressed by the hunger and fatigues we had suffered, now almost entirely sunk within us, feeling no resource left, nor any reasonable ground to hope that we should escape a most miserable death by famine."

Quickly Rogers regained control and came up with a plan. Leaving most of his starving men behind, Rogers and two men left to get help from the British Fort No. 4. Rogers promised his men that they would have food in ten days.

Rogers and his two men left on October 27. Rogers knew that traveling on the river was the only way to make it to No. 4. They had no energy left to walk. Making a raft from pine logs, the three Rangers let the wild, frothy river take them. They had to get past two waterfalls during their trip. At the first, they lost their raft, and barely had the strength to build another. At the second waterfall, they threw themselves off the raft and swam to shore, dragging the raft with them. Rogers then ran below the falls and swam out into freezing water to retrieve the raft, while Captain Ogden, who was traveling with him, lowered the raft carefully using rope made from hazel twigs. Rogers reached No. 4 in four days. Food was sent out immediately and arrived exactly when Rogers had promised: ten days after he had left.

The attack on St. Francis was one of Rogers' most difficult assignments. He lost forty-nine men, seventeen from battle and thirty-two from starvation. His brave effort to save his men when his own army had deserted him proved that Robert Rogers was truly a hero.

8. Fighting Canada (1760)

The Rangers and the Isle aux Noix

In 1760, the British had a third threefold plan to beat the French. The British had already taken the French city Quebec, and they now had their eyes set on Montreal. The British knew they were very close to winning the war. Rogers and his Rangers were to help General Haviland move northward through the Champlain Valley and the Richelieu River toward Montreal and be ready to fight.

On August 11, led by Haviland, 3,400 British soldiers and six hundred Rangers left Crown Point. They arrived near the Isle aux Noix, an island in the Richelieu River, almost a week later. Fighting began between the British and French warships in the middle of the afternoon on August 23. The British fired cannon shots and it was not long before the French fled for safety.

The British noticed a French boat escaping the battle, paddling down the Richelieu River. Rogers and his Rangers were immediately sent after it. The Rangers

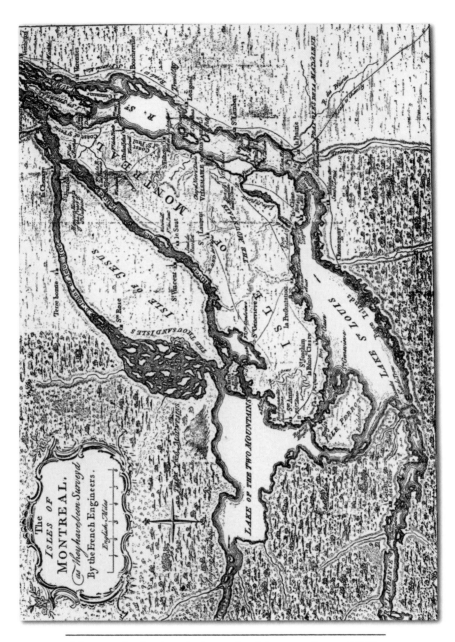

Montreal, depicted above in this map from 1761, was one of the last French possessions, or cities, unconquered by the British.

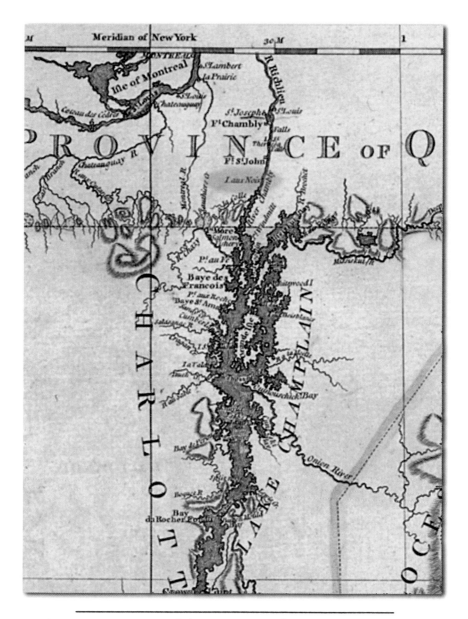

This is a 1776 map of the provinces of New York and Quebec.
The green oval at the top of map is Isle aux Noix.
The British soldiers and Rangers marched for a week
to reach Isle aux Noix, and attacked on August 23, 1760.

were up to the task, as always. A group of Rangers took off their clothes and most of their equipment, jumped into the water with their tomahawks between their teeth, and swam after the disappearing boat. By the time they had reached the boat and climbed on board, the French were so scared that they surrendered right away. Once again, the Rangers proved how valuable their method of fighting was.

Although Haviland and the Rangers were there if they were needed, it was Amherst's army that sur-rounded the city and took control. On September 8, the French surrendered Montreal to the British. Robert Rogers wrote in his journals: "At the end of the fifth campaign, Montreal and the whole country of Canada was given up, and became subject to the King of Great Britain; a conquest perhaps of the greatest importance that is to be met with in the British annals. . . . "

Robert Rogers Carries the British Flag West

Robert Rogers had one last assignment before he completed his days of being the commander of the Rangers. Following the French surrender at Montreal, Amherst asked Rogers to carry the British flag west to Detroit and to all of the western French posts. He was to show the French soldiers at the western outposts a letter proving that the French had indeed surrendered. Rogers was then supposed to collect the French soldiers'

Robert Rogers' final job in the French and Indian War was to carry the British flag west. The flag used in the colonies at this time was the British Union Jack. The flag design was created by King James VI of Scotland when he became king of England in 1603. It was created by combining England's red cross of St. George with Scotland's white cross of St. Andrew.

weapons and ask the French to support the British. Rogers also would need to make peace with the Indians who had allied with the French during the war.

Rogers was an excellent choice for this mission, and it was a job he welcomed. Not only was Rogers the perfect man to travel into the unknown wilderness, but he also understood how to interact with the Indian culture more than most other British soldiers.

Rogers left Montreal in daylight on September 13, 1760. He stopped at many outposts along the way,

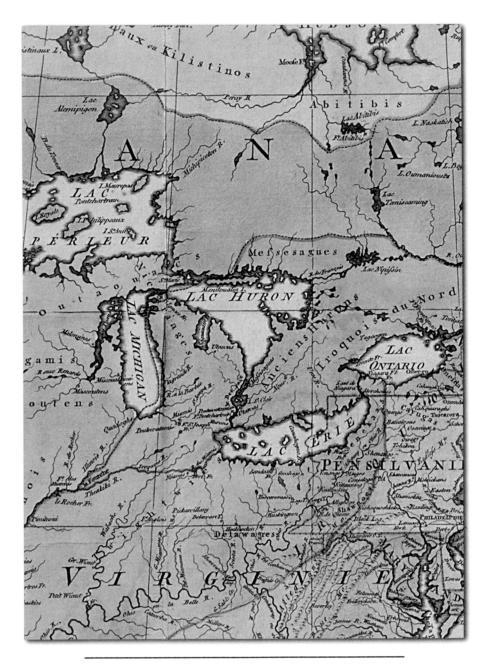

This 1755 map shows the area from Montreal to the western end of Lake Erie that Robert Rogers visited on his way to Detroit. Although there were settlements scattered throughout the West at this time, it was largely wilderness. Rogers was chosen for his ability to navigate easily through rough terrain.

spreading the word of Britain's victory. A little more than two months later, Rogers finally arrived at the western end of Lake Erie, close to the fort of Detroit. He asked one of his men to carry a letter to the French commander of Detroit to inform him of the French surrender. Although Rogers' messenger had given the letter to the French commander, a group of Indians appeared at Rogers' camp, armed with weapons. The Indians were French allies. They said there were four hundred more Indians waiting to stop the British from passing farther and that their French leader had told them that they could defend their country if the new British rule was not true. They wanted proof from Robert Rogers that the French surrender was real. Rogers proved the French surrender by showing them a copy of the letter.

Upon Robert Rogers' arrival in Detroit, he called a meeting between the British and the chiefs of the nearby Indian tribes. At these meetings, each person introduced themselves and the British explained the purpose of their arrival. The Indians met within their own tribes to discuss the news and weigh their options, which were either to fight or to agree to the British terms. The Indians returned in support of the new rulers. Following this discussion, all the parties exchanged gifts, smoked peace pipes, and drank rum to celebrate.

On November 29, 1760, the local Indians, the French soldiers, and the British soldiers gathered around, and the British flag was raised in Detroit to a general cheer. The British controlled the West.

Although fighting in North America was done, the official end to the war would not come until three years later. The Treaty of Paris, which would formally end the French and Indian War, was signed in 1763.

9. After the War (1760–1795)

Robert Rogers and his Debts

Robert Rogers was plagued by debts throughout his life. Because he and his Rangers were independent companies of the British army rather than a part of the permanent establishment, Rogers and his Rangers did not always get the money that they were promised from the British government. This happened for a few different reasons. Rogers often paid his Rangers using his own money, expecting reimbursement from the government at a later time. The government did not always pay. In part, this was because Rogers did not keep good enough records to satisfy his superiors. The other reason was that some members of the British government, especially Sir William Johnson and General Thomas Gage, did not like Rogers and they felt they could get away without paying him.

Even though the British government did not pay Rogers what he was owed, he still needed money to live. People allowed him to borrow the goods and services he needed, and he promised to pay them back. Rogers ended up in debt. The people collecting money, called creditors, were always after Rogers to pay what he owed. Unfortunately, he often did not have the money to repay what he had borrowed. At that time, if you did not pay your debts you were placed in debtor's prison. Rogers spent much of his life after the war in and out of debtor's prison, struggling to make money to live.

Rogers also made several trips to England during the course of his life to plead for payment. Between his constant debt and the many foes who had never liked him or his Rangers, many people on both sides of the Atlantic Ocean believed Rogers was not an honorable

Above is an illustration depicting a English debtor's prison. In the eighteenth century, the English penal code called for the imprisonment of citizens who had fallen behind in their private debts. One was kept in the debtor's prison until a friend or family member could pay off the debt.

man. These trips to England also created another problem for Rogers. When he wanted to fight for American independence at the outbreak of the American Revolution, George Washington would not allow him to enter his camp because he thought that Rogers was a spy. In the end, Rogers ended up fighting for the British and became a loyalist leader, which would not help his reputation in America.

Robert Rogers Takes a Wife

In 1755, when Robert Rogers was just beginning his successful career as a Ranger, he was inducted into the Masonic Lodge in Portsmouth, New Hampshire. The Masons, also known as Freemasons, were a group of men, or a brotherhood, that had secret rituals and whose purpose was to support, defend, and protect one another. It was an honor for Rogers to be asked. Some of the most important men in the community were a part of this group. In fact, the chaplain of the lodge was Reverend Arthur Browne, a rector at a local church. Reverend Browne had a fourteen-year-old daughter named Elizabeth who had noticed Robert Rogers, a "famous" hero who had defended the frontier's dangerous borders.

Rogers went back to city life when the fighting in the French and Indian War ended in 1760, and he had finished his mission to the western outposts in 1761. He became reacquainted with Elizabeth Browne, who was

This portrait of George Washington was done by James Peale in 1760. Washington, who led the American forces, did not trust Rogers and refused his help in America's war for independence. Rogers would eventually fight for the British in a losing cause.

then twenty years old. Robert Rogers fell in love. Rogers and Elizabeth were married on June 30, 1761. They had one son together, named Arthur, who was baptized on February 12, 1769.

Because of his debts, Rogers did not have much money to support his wife. Sometimes he had no money at all. To make a living, Rogers often left home, heading to the outskirts of the frontier to find work as a speculator. During their marriage, Rogers and Elizabeth often were separated, although Elizabeth sometimes went to the wilderness with him. She was not happy with either situation. Between Robert's lack of finances and their living situation, their marriage was in trouble. Finally, after seventeen years, Elizabeth filed for divorce on February 11, 1778.

Robert Rogers Writes

In 1765, Robert Rogers published the *Journals of Major Robert Rogers*. The book, which was quoted from in this book, was a first-person account of his duties and experience in the French and Indian War. It described some of the most important battles that the Rangers fought, and covered both the high points and the low points of the war. His journals were popular because both the British settlers and the people in England could read it and find out what it was really like in the wilderness and, more particularly, what

This is a painting of Elizabeth Browne Rogers, Rogers' wife, done by I. Blackburn Pinxit in 1761. Robert and his wife spent a great deal of time apart and struggled financially. The marriage ended in divorce after seventeen years.

it was like on the battlefields of North America.

At the time it was published, people realized Robert Rogers' words were important. Today, this is one of the best firsthand accounts of what life was like in the early eighteenth century that is still available.

The second book that Rogers published was called *A Concise Account of North America*, and it was even more popular than his journals. Rogers was one of the first men to experience and come to know the wild frontier of America. In this book, he shared what he knew and what he had learned. The British were very interested in this book because the new land of North America was still a foreign place. Most British people, including the leaders of the country, had never been to America. They had only heard about it. Rogers' book let them read and imagine what this wild place was really like.

There is also a third book that people think Rogers wrote, though he never claimed it was his. It was a play named *Ponteach, or the Savages of America*. Ponteach was the famous Indian Chief Pontiac. The book described the conversations and negotiations between the British and the Indians. People did not like the book. It described how the British treated the Indians badly, and painted the behavior of the British in a very negative light. Perhaps this is why Rogers never took ownership of it.

The quest for the Northwest Passage across the American continent had been going on for as long as people were settled in America. It was hoped that there was a water route from the Atlantic Ocean to the Pacific Ocean that would open up a direct trade route to the Orient. Such a route would also have been useful in trade between North American settlements. Rogers believed that he would find the Northwest Passage by going across the Great Lakes. If he had received the necessary funding, Rogers would have been the first to cross the continent in the same area that Lewis and Clark would travel forty years later.

Robert Rogers and the Northwest Passage

In 1766, Robert Rogers wanted to lead a trip through the wilderness to explore Britain's new territories and to discover the Northwest Passage. What Rogers really hoped was that he could find a way to make money and escape from under his pile of debts. He did not know what he would find, but perhaps it would be animal skins that he could sell for a lot of money, or perhaps he would find a water route, which would promote trading across the continent to the Pacific Ocean. Rogers hoped, of course, to find both things. Unfortunately, he never made the trip.

Rogers estimated that the trip would take three

years and asked the British government to give him money to pay for the trip. The British government did not have money to spare. It was expensive to protect the borders of Britain's new North American land. Britain kept soldiers at various points along the borders because they did not want the Indians or the French to try to take back North America. Rogers could not afford to fund the trip himself.

Rogers also could not go on the search because he had just been made governor of Michilimackinac, and his duties kept him there. Although Rogers did

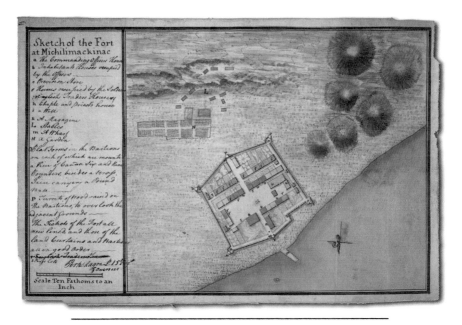

This is a depiction of Fort Michilimackinac by Lieutentant Perkins Magra. Rogers was made governor of Michilimackinac in 1766. Rogers' duties as governor kept him from traveling in search of the Northwest Passage, which had been a dream of his for years. Without Rogers' guidance, the men he had ordered to go in his place quickly gave up the search.

not go in search of the Northwest Passage, in 1767 a group of British under Rogers' orders went to explore and see what they could. The men returned quickly, saying they could not find the Northwest Passage and had given up. Rogers was devastated. He believed that if he had gone the men would have kept trying and he would have been able to find it. Robert Rogers tried to get funding for a Northwest Passage expedition up until the start of the American Revolution, but he never received any money.

Robert Rogers was buried at a churchyard near an inn called the Elephant and Castle. In fact, this whole section was called the Elephant and Castle. Apparently the inn was converted from a smithy in the 1760s and was at a crossroads called the Elephant. Presumably the inn took its name from this. This lithograph of the crossroads was done by James Pollard after an aquatint by Theodore Fielding.

Robert Rogers Dies

On May 18, 1795, at age sixty-four, Robert Rogers died in London, England, from an unknown illness. His last years were spent in extreme hardship. He was never able to get out from under his debts. On May 20, Rogers was buried at a churchyard near an inn called the Elephant and Castle. The obituary in a local newspaper read: "Lieutenant Col. Rogers, who died on Thursday last in the Borough [of London], served in America during the late war, in which he performed prodigious feats of valor. He was a man of uncommon strength . . ."

10. Robert Rogers' Legacy

The French and Indian War was an important war in America's history. For seven long years, two of Europe's great nations battled for control of North America. Many lives were lost on both sides. Though the Revolutionary War is often thought to be America's first war, it really was not. In fact many of the Revolutionary War heroes, like George Washington, who went on to become America's first president, had their first battle experience in the French and Indian War.

What would have happened if the French had won the French and Indian War? The North American continent would have grown up as a French colony, not a British one. It is hard to imagine how our entire American history would have changed.

There is no doubt that Robert Rogers was not only one of the most famous people fighting for the British during the French and Indian War, but he was also one of America's first heroes.

Robert Rogers had been brave and strong for his whole life, even as a young man. He recognized his love

This is the monument to Rogers' Rangers on Rogers Island at Fort Edward, New York. An important part of the British war effort during the French and Indian War, ranging companies, like Rogers' men, would continue to play a vital role as part of America's defenses in wars to come.

for America's wilderness and he followed his dreams. He converted the hardships he had faced as a child into skills to shape a life he understood. Although he did not always make the right choices, he acted honorably and served his country. He defended his American homeland as best he could.

As a soldier and a Ranger, Robert Rogers helped to perfect a new way of fighting in the British army. He was able to gather information from living in the American wilderness and his understanding of the

This engraving depicts the wilderness as it
probably looked during Robert Rogers' lifetime.
There were dense forests, mountains, lakes, and
thousands of miles of uncharted territory.

Indian culture. Armed with this knowledge, he created a set of rules called "Rogers' Rules of Ranging," that forever changed the way wars would be fought. In fact, these rules are still taught in the military today.

He built a company from scratch. He taught an entire group of fighters a way of doing battle in the American terrain. Eventually the method spread into all areas of the British attack against the French and Indians. Had it not been for Robert Rogers' knowledge, strength, and bravery, Britain might have lost the French and Indian War, and North America would have been a French nation. Rogers truly helped to shape the America we live in today.

Appendix

Rogers' Rules of Ranging

Robert Rogers wrote rules for his rangers to follow. These rules are still in use today. Here are "Rogers' Rules for Ranging" written in 1757:

1.) All Rangers are to be subject to the rules and articles of war; to appear at roll-call every evening on their own parade, equipped, each with a firelock, sixty rounds of powder and ball, and a hatchet, at which time an officer from each company is to inspect the same, to see they are in order, so as to be ready on any emergency to march at a minute's warning: and before they are dismissed the necessary guards are to be draughted, and scouts for the next day appointed.

2.) Whenever you are ordered out to the enemy's forts or frontiers for discoveries, if your number be small, march in a single file, keeping at such a distance from each other as to prevent one shot from killing two men, sending one man, or more, forward, and the like on each side, at the distance of twenty yards from the main body. If the ground you march over will admit of it, to give the signal to the officer of the approach of an enemy and their number, &c.

3.) If you march over marshes or soft ground, change your position and march abreast of each other to prevent the enemy from tracking you, (as they would do if you marched in a single file), till you get over such ground, and then resume your former order, and march till it is quite dark before you encamp, which do, if possible, on a piece of ground that may afford your sentries the advantage of seeing or hearing the enemy at some considerable distance, keeping one half of your whole party awake alternately through the night.

4.) Some time before you come to the place you would reconnoitre, make a stand and send one or two men in whom you can confide, to look out the best ground for making your observations.

5.) If you have the good fortune to take any prisoners, keep them separate till they are examined, and in your return take a different route from that in which you went out, that you may better discover any party in your rear, and have an opportunity, if their strength be superior to yours, to alter your course, or disperse, as circumstances may require.

6.) If you march in a large body of three or four hundred, with a design to attack the enemy, divide your party into three columns, each headed by a proper officer, and let these columns march in single files, the columns to the right and left keeping at twenty yards distance or more from that of the center, if the ground will admit, and let proper guards be kept in the front and rear, and suitable flanking parties at a due distance as before directed, with orders to halt on all eminences, to take a view of the surrounding ground, to prevent your being ambuscaded, and to notify the approach or retreat of the enemy, that proper dispositions may be made for attacking, defending, &c. And if the enemy approach in your front on level ground, form a front of your three columns or main body with the advanced guard, keeping your flanking parties, as if you were marching under the command of trusty officers, to prevent the enemy from pressing hard on either of your wings, or surrounding you, which is the usual method of the savages, if their number will admit of it, and be careful likewise to support and strengthen your rear-guard.

7.) If you are obliged to receive the enemy's fire, fall, or squat down, till it is over, then rise and discharge at them. If their main body is equal to yours, extend yourselves occasionally; but if superior, be careful to support and strengthen your flanking parties, to make them equal to theirs, that if possible you may repulse them to their main body, in which case push upon them with the greatest resolution, with equal force in each flank and in the center, observing to keep at a due distance from each other, and advance from tree to tree, with one half of the party before the other ten or twelve yards. If the enemy push upon you, let your front fire and fall down, and then let your rear advance through them and do the like, by which time those who before were in front will be ready to discharge again, and repeat the same alternately, as occasion shall require by this means you will keep up such a constant fire, that the enemy will not be able easily to break your order, or gain your ground.

8.) If you oblige the enemy to retreat, be careful, in your pursuit of them, to keep out your flanking parties, and present them from gaining eminences, or rising grounds, in which case they would perhaps be able to rally and repulse you in their turn.

9.) If you are obliged to retreat, let the front of your whole party fire and fall back, till the rear hath done the same, making for the best ground you can; by this means you will oblige the enemy to pursue you, if they do it at all, in the face of constant fire.

10.) If the enemy is so superior that you are in danger of being surrounded by them, let the whole body disperse, and everyone take a different road to the place of rendezvous appointed for that evening, which must every morning be altered and fixed for the evening ensuing, in order to bring the whole party, or as many of them as possible, together, after any separation, that may happen in the day; but if you should happen to be actually surrounded, form yourselves into a square, or if in the woods, a circle is best, and if possible, make a stand till the darkness of the night favours your escape.

11.) If your rear is attacked, the main body and flankers must face about to the right or left, as occasion shall require and form themselves to oppose the enemy, as before directed; and the same method must be observed, if attacked in either of your flanks, by which means you will always make a rear of one of your flank-guards.

12.) If you determine to rally after retreat, in order to make a fresh stand against the enemy, by all means endeavor to do it on the most rising ground you come at, which will give you greatly the advantage in point of situation, and enable you to repulse superior numbers.

13.) In general, when pushed upon by the enemy, reserve your fire till they approach very near, which will then put them into the greatest surprize and consternation, and give you an opportunity of rushing upon them with your hatchets and cutlasses to the better advantage.

14.) When you encamp at night, fix your sentries in such a manner as not to be relieved from the main body till morning, profound secrecy and silence being often of the last importance in these cases. Each sentry, therefore, should consist of six men, two of whom must be constantly alert, and when relieved by their fellows, it should be done without noise; and in case those on duty see or hear anything, which alarms them, they are not to speak, but one of them is silently to retreat, and acquaint the commanding officer thereof, that proper dispositions may be made; and all occasional sentries should be fixed in like manner.

15.) At the first dawn of day, awake your whole detachment; that being the time when the savages chuse to fall upon their enemies, you should by all means be in readiness to receive them.

16.) If the enemy should be discovered by your detachments in the morning, and their numbers are superior to yours, and a victory is doubtful, you should not attack them till the evening, as then they will not know your numbers, and if you are repulsed, your retreat will be favoured by the darkness of night.

17.) Before you leave your encampment, send out small parties to scout round it, to see if there be any appearance or track of an enemy that might have been near you during the night.

18.) When you stop for refreshment, chuse some spring or rivulet if you can, and dispose your party so as not to be surprised, posting proper guards and sentries at a due distance, and let a small party waylay the path you came in, lest the enemy should be pursuing.

19.) If, in your return, you have to cross rivers, avoid the usual fords as much as possible, lest the enemy should have discovered, and be there expecting you.

20.) If you have to pass by lakes, keep at some distance from the edge of the water, lest, in case of an ambuscade or an attack from the enemy, when in that situation, your retreat should be cut off.

21.) If the enemy pursue your rear, take a circle till you come to your own tracks, and there form an ambush to receive them, and give them first fire.

22.) When you return from a scout, and come near our forts, avoid the usual roads, and avenues thereto, lest the enemy should have headed you, and lay in ambush to receive you, when almost exhausted with fatigues.

23.) When you pursue any party that has been near our forts or encampments, follow not directly in their tracks, lest you should be discovered by their rear-guards, who, at such time, would be most alert; but endeavor, by a different route, to head and meet them in some narrow pass, or lay in ambush to receive them when and where they least expect it.

24.) If you are to embark in canoes, battoes, or otherwise, by water, chuse the evening for the time of embarkation, as you will then have the whole night before you, to pass undiscovered by any parties of the enemy, on hills, or other places, which command a prospect of the lake or river you are upon.

25.) In padling or rowing, give orders that the boat or canoe next the sternmost, wait for her, and the third for the second, and the fourth for the third, and so on, to prevent separation, and that you may be ready to assist each other on any emergency.

26.) Appoint one man in each boat to look out for fires on the adjacent shores, from the numbers and size of which you may form some judgment of the number that kindled them, and whether you are able to attack them or not.

27.) If you find the enemy encamped near the banks of the river, or lake, which you imagine they will attempt to cross for their security upon being attacked, leave a detachment of your party on the opposite shore to receive them, while with the remainder, you surprize them, having them between you and the lake or river.

28.) If you cannot satisfy yourself as to the enemy's number and strength, from their fire, &c., conceal your boats at some distance, and ascertain their number by a reconnoitring party, when they embark, or march, in the morning, marking the course they steer, &c., when you may pursue, ambush, and attack them, or let them pass, as prudence shall direct you. In general, however, that you may not be discovered by the enemy on the lakes and rivers at a great distance, it is safest to lay by, with your boats and party concealed all day, without noise or shew, and to pursue your intended route by night; and whether you go by land or by water, give out parole and countersigns, in order to know one another in the dark, and likewise appoint a station for every man to repair to, in case of any accident that may separate you.

29.) If you are attacked in flat or rough ground, retreat in a scattering method and let the enemy believe you are routed until you come to an advantageous spot, then allow the enemy to come close and deliver a volley, and immediately after, the men nearest to them rush upon them with hatchets, and the rest to surround their flanks in their confusion.

Such in general are the rules to be observed in the Ranging service; there are, however, a thousand occurrences and circumstances which may happen, that will make it necessary, in some measure to depart from them, and to put other arts and stratagems in practice; in which cases every man's reason and judgment must be his guide, according to the particular situation and nature of things; and that he may do this to advantage, he should keep in mind a maxim never to be departed from by a commander, viz. To preserve a firmness and presence of mind on every occasion.

Timeline

1731	On November 18, Robert Rogers is born in Methuen, Massachusetts.
1738	The Rogers family purchases land in New Hampshire.
1745	French-led Indian attacks begin in the English frontier. Robert becomes a militiaman.
1748	A group of Indians raid and attack the Rogers' family home.
1753	The French and Indian War begins.
1755	In February, Robert Rogers is caught passing counterfeit money. Robert Rogers recruits fifty men to join him to fight in the French and Indian War. On September 14, Rogers and four men go on their first scouting mission.

On September 27, Rogers leads his second scouting mission where, behind enemy lines, he attacks the enemy, takes prisoners, and becomes a hero.

1757   Lord George Augustus Viscount Howe is made a brigadier in North America.

In December, the Mutiny of the Whipping Post occurs.

1758   On March 10, Rogers' Rangers leave Rogers Island near Fort Edward and fight in the battle known as the Battle on Snowshoes.

On April 6, Rogers is promoted from captain to major.

In July, Lord Howe is killed.

In December, Jeffrey Amherst takes over for General Abercromby.

1759   On July 22, the British army leaves Fort George to try to take Fort Carillon.

On September 13, Rogers and his men set out to attack the St. Francis Indians.

	On October 5, the British attack on St. Francis occurs.
1760	August 23, 1760 Fighting begins at Isle Aux Noix.
	On September 13, Rogers begins his journey west carrying the British flag.
	On November 29, the British flag is raised in Detroit. The British control the West.
1761	June 30, 1761 Robert Rogers marries Elizabeth Browne.
1763	The Treaty of Paris is signed, formally ending the French and Indian War.
1765	Robert Rogers publishes the *Journals of Major Robert Rogers*.
1767	A group of men, not including Rogers, leave to find the Northwest Passage.
1769	On February 12, Robert Rogers' only son, Arthur, is born.
1778	On February 11, Elizabeth Rogers files for divorce from Robert Rogers.
1795	On May 18, Robert Rogers dies in London, England.

Glossary

allies (A-lyz) Groups of people that agree to work together.

ambush (AM-bush) A trap in which people hide and lie in wait to attack by surprise.

ammunition (am-yoo-NIH-shun) The materials used for attacking or defending a position, such as the bullets or other items fired from guns.

barrels (BAHR-ulz) The cylindrical part of a gun where the ammunition comes out.

bateau (ba-TOH) A flat-bottomed boat that usually has flared sides.

battery (BA-tur-ree) A protected position for cannon.

bayonets (BAY-oh-netz) Knives on the end of weapons.

blanket-coats (BLAYN-keht-KOHTS) Blankets cut and sewn together to make hooded coats.

branding (BRAND-ing) A mark burned into the skin.

brutally (BROO-tuh-lee) To attack cruelly or in cold-blood. A behavior that is enacted savagely or without feeling.

canteen (kan-TEEN) A container that is used to hold liquid; a water bottle.

citadel (SIT-ah-del) A stronghold or fortress that usually commands or protects a city.

conflict (KON-flikt) A fight, battle, or war between two people or groups.

counterfeit money (KOWN-tur-fit MUH-nee) Money that is illegally made, not real money.

desert (dih-ZURT) To illegally leave government employment during a war.

eminence (EH-mih-nents) A position of prominence or superiority, in this case which provides a better view of something.

fife (FYF) A small flute that is held to the side instead of straight out from the mouth.

flask (FLASK) A type of bottle used to carry a variety of liquids.

flogged (FLAWGD) To be beaten with a whip, often one made of leather.

haversack (HAV-ur-sak) A rectangular pouch with a flap, carried by the Rangers.

heritage (HER-ih-tij) The cultural traditions passed from parent to child.

immigrated (IH-muh-grayted) Moved from one country to another.

militiaman (mih-LIH-shuh-mun) A citizen from a community that fights to protect the community form harm.

mutiny (MYOO-tin-ee) A riot or rebellion by a group against lawful authority or a superior officer.

obituary (oh-BIH-choo-wer-ee) A death notice often found in a newspaper.

outskirts (OWT-skerts) A part or place far from the center; especially of town. A place at the very edge of town.

pillaged (PIL-ijd) The act of looting, or plundering ruthlessly, or to ravage or destroy something.

provisions (pruh-VIH-zhuns) Food and supplies.

rations (RA-shunz) Food given to people in controlled amounts which is meant to last for a certain amount of time.

reality (ree-A-lih-tee) The true situation.

recruit (ree-KROOT) To convince people to join your group.

rendezvous (RAN-dih-voo) A place agreed upon for meeting; or a meeting at a specified place and time.

retaliate (rih-TA-lee-ayt) To get back at someone for something done to you.

scalping knife (SKALP-ing NYF) A long, thin hunting knife, which was used to remove the scalp of an enemy.

skirmish (SKUR-mish) To have small fights.

terrain (tuh-RAYN) A piece of land or the physical qualities of a piece of land.

uncouth (un-KOOTH) Awkward and uncultivated in manner, appearance, or behavior, or lacking in grace or polish.

uncultivated (un-KUL-tuh-vayt-ed) Something that is rough or wild. Land that has not been farmed.

whipping post (WIP-ping POHST) A tall log where disobedient Rangers would be punished.

Additional Resources

To learn more about Robert Rogers, the Rangers, and the French and Indian War, check out these books and Web sites.

Books

Collier, Christopher, and James Lincoln Collier. *The French and Indian War: 1660–1763 (Drama of American History)*. Washington, DC: Benchmark Books, 1998.

Maestro, Betsy C., and Giulio Maestro (illustrator). *Struggle for a Continent: The French and Indian Wars 1689–1763*. New York: HarperCollins Juvenile Books, 2000.

Reeder, Colonel Red. *The French & Indian War*. Quechee, VT: The Fort Ticonderoga Association and Vermont Heritage Press, 1997.

Smith, Bradford. *Robert Rogers and the French and Indian War*. New York: Random House, 1956.

Web Sites

www.rogersrangers.com
www.rrangers.org

Bibliography

Cuneo, John R. *Robert Rogers of the Rangers*. New York: Fort Ticonderoga Museum, 1988.

Loescher, Burt Garfield. *The History of Rogers' Rangers, Volume I: The Beginnings, January 1755–April 6, 1758*. California: Published privately by the author, 1946.

Parkman, Francis. *The Battle for North America*. New York: Doubleday & Company, 1948.

Peckham, Howard H. *The Colonial Wars 1689–1972*. Chicago: The University of Chicago Press, 1995.

Rogers, Major Robert. *Journals of Major Robert Rogers (London 1765)*. Bargersville, Indiana: Dresslar Publishing, 1997.

Schwartz, Seymour I. *The French and Indian War 1754–1763: The Imperial Struggle for North America*. New York: Castle Books, 1994.

Scott, Kenneth. *Counterfeiting in Colonial America*. New York: Oxford University Press, 1957.

Todish, Timothy J. *America's First World War: The French and Indian War 1754–1763*. Fleischmonns, NY: Purple Mountain Press, 2001.

Index

About the Author

Jennifer Quasha is a writer and editor living in New York City. Also a skilled researcher, Jennifer has written six social studies and history books for children along with nine books for both school and library and trade publishers. She has edited many natural history books including *Walking with Dinosaurs* and *Cousins* for the BBC/DK Publishing. Taking on Robert Rogers was a welcome challenge, as Jennifer researched and unearthed primary documents relating to Rogers and the War and then wrote about the larger-than-life hero.

About the Consultant

Timothy J. Todish is an historical writer and consultant specializing in Robert Rogers and the French and Indian War. He has written several books including: *America's FIRST First World War: The French and Indian War 1754–1763, Alamo Sourcebook 1836: A Comprehensive Guide to the Alamo and the Texas Revolution*, and is working with artist Gary Zaboly on a footnoted and illustrated edition of *Robert Rogers' JOURNALS*. Timothy was also the technical adviser for the award-winning History Channel series *Frontier: Legends of the Old Northwest* and a consultant for the Learning Channel series *Archaeology* and the PBS series *Anyplace Wild*.

Credits

Photo Credits

Pp. 4, 11, 20, 72 © 1999 Corbis; p. 6 Corinne Jacob; p. 8 © Bettmann/CORBIS; p. 12 © Roman Soumar/CORBIS; pp. 15, 47 © SuperStock; pp. 23, 61 © Lee Snider; Lee Snider/CORBIS; p. 24 Courtesy, Winterthur Museum; p. 27 © Arthur D'Arazien/SuperStock; pp. 28, 38 (top) Collections of the Fort Ticonderoga Museum; pp. 30, 45, 68, 71 © North Wind Picture Archives p. 32 Courtesy Gary F. Zaboly; pp. 34-35, 50, 69 courtesy of Map Division, The New York Public Library, Astor, Lenox and Tilden Foundations; p. 38 (middle, bottom left, and bottom right); © National Museum of American History, Smithsonian Institution; p. 41 Collection of the New-York Historical Society; p. 42 © Clemens Library, The University of Michigan; p. 44 © Christie's Images, Ltd. 2001; pp. 52-53, 62 © Prints George; p. 55 © The British Museum; pp. 56, 87 Courtesy, Timothy J. Todish; p. 57 Courtesy, Aquarian Gallery; p. 76 © Baldwin H. Ward & Kathryn C. Ward/CORBIS; p. 78 © CORBIS; p. 80 © Reynolda House, Museum of American Art, Winston-Salem, North Carolina, 1967.07.31.00; p. 83 © Clemens Library, The University of Michigan; p. 84 © Mary Evans Picture Library; p. 88 © Archive Photos.

Series Design

Laura Murawski

Layout Design

Corinne Jacob

Project Editor

Joanne Randolph